My First Time

Staying
Overnight

Kate Petty, Lisa Kopper, and Jim Pipe

Stargazer Books

Designed and produced by
Aladdin Books Ltd

First published in 2008
in the United States by
Stargazer Books
c/o The Creative Company
123 South Broad Street
Mankato, Minnesota 56002

Printed in the United States

Illustrator: Lisa Kopper

Photocredits:
All photos from istockphoto.com except 16—Ingram Publishing.

Library of Congress Cataloging-in-Publication Data

Petty, Kate.
  Staying overnight / by Kate Petty.
      p. cm. -- (My first time)
  Summary: Sam is excited to stay over at his friend Tom's house, and the fun he has, along with the
kindness of Tom's parents and older sister, more than make up for the few things he does not like.
    ISBN 978-1-59604-156-1 (alk. paper)
    [1. Sleepovers--Fiction.] I. Title.
  PZ7.P44814Sta 2007
  [E]--dc22
                              2007001767

About this book

New experiences can be scary for young children. This series will help them to understand situations they may find themselves in, by explaining in a friendly way what can happen.

This book can be used as a starting point for discussing issues. The questions in some of the boxes ask children about their own experiences.

The stories will also help children to master basic reading skills and learn new vocabulary.

It can help if you read the first sentence to children, and then encourage them to read the rest of the page or story. At the end, try looking through the book again to find where the words in the glossary are used.

Contents

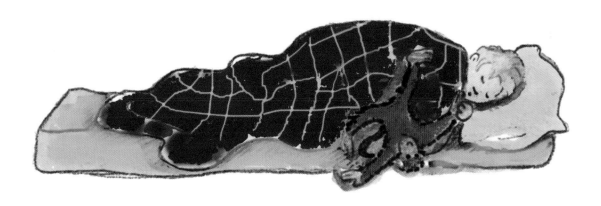

Sam's going to stay with his friend Tom.
It's the first time he's been away
from Mom and Dad for a whole night.

"Don't forget Monkey, Sam," says Dad.

4

Tom's mom is called Jane. "Hello, Sam. We're going to enjoy your visit."

Sam just remembers to wave goodbye before Tom pulls him into the house.

What would you pack your clothes in?

Tom really wants to show Sam his toys.
"That's where you're going to sleep."

Sam hasn't slept on the floor before.
But the mattress feels springy and soft.

Tom and Sam both bounce on the beds.
Whoops! What a mess they've made!

Tom's big sister, Alice, looks in.
Is she mad? No, there's no harm done.

It's supper time. Sam sits by Tom.
Oh dear. It's fishsticks tonight.

"Everyone likes fishsticks," says Alice.
Sam wishes they'd just disappear.

What do you
like for supper?

Jane makes peanut butter sandwiches.
Sam could eat a whole plateful of these.

And there's ice cream for dessert.
Sam enjoys his supper after all.

Jane runs a bath, steamy and deep.
Tom adds some bubblebath.

Sam had brought his best bath toys.
It's time to have some fun!

They play some very splashy games.
"I think you two had better help
to mop up this water," says Jane.
Cleaning up is quite fun too.

Sam needs some help with his pyjamas.
Will Alice laugh at him?

But Alice was once a little girl
who needed help too.

12

How often should you brush your teeth?

Tom guards the door while Sam is in the bathroom. Don't let anyone in!

One more thing to do before bed. "I like your toothpaste, Tom."

13

Sam has brought his favorite books.
Where has Monkey gone?

Sam wonders if Alice has hidden him.
But Alice doesn't know where Monkey is.

14

Alice looks everywhere.
Here he is!

Then she offers
to read to them.
Sam chooses a book
and she reads all of it.
Tom is lucky to have a big sister.

15

Does a teddy
help you sleep?

Sam has a nightlight at home.
He hopes he can sleep without it.

Alice leaves the landing light on.
"Call if you want anything, Sam."

16

Tom wants everything.
Another story, a drink, a snack…

"Go to sleep now, Tom," whispers Jane.
"Look. Sam is fast asleep already."

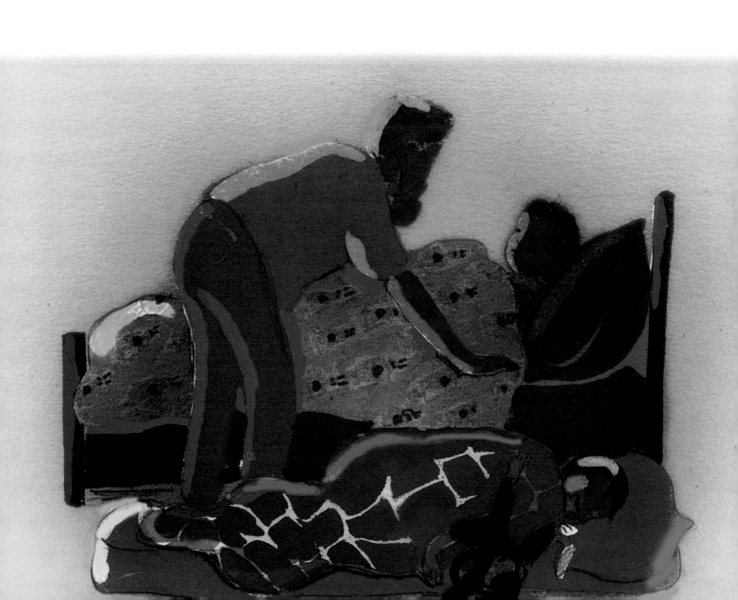

Sam wakes up in the middle of the night.
It seems very dark and strange.

It's scary when everyone else is asleep.
"Jane!" calls Sam.

"Poor Sam," says Jane and cuddles him.

She fixes up the nightlight that Alice used to have. Sam can sleep now. "Goodnight."

A lamp lights up a dark room.

19

The children are up first in the morning.
"Who wants ice cream for breakfast?"
asks Alice. Sam and Tom want some.

Jane has other ideas about breakfast.

Mom, Dad, and Jenny come to pick up Sam.
But Sam doesn't want to go yet.

"Never mind, Sam. You must come again."
"Thank you for having me," says Sam.

bag

bouncing on the beds

pyjamas

bath time

reading
a story

sleeping

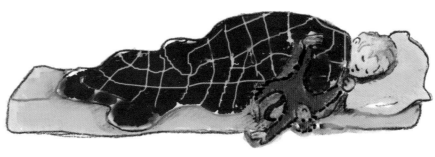

nightlight

Index

Find out more

Find out more about organizing a sleepover:

http://summer.about.com/od/craftsfunactivities/ht/slumberparty.htm
http://parentcenter.babycenter.com/expert/preschooler/pdevelopment/70282.html
http://www.parents.com/parents/story.jhtml?storyid=/templatedata/parents/story/data/3212.xml&catref=prt23